CORAL REEF FOOD CHAINS

Kelley MacAulay & Bobbie Kalman

Crabtree Publishing Company

www.crabtreebooks.com

Coral Reef Food Chains

Created by Bobbie Kalman

Dedicated by Kelley MacAulay
For Emilie MacAulay and Jennifer Desrosiers, with love

Editor-in-Chief
Bobbie Kalman

Writing team
Kelley MacAulay
Bobbie Kalman

Substantive editor
Kathryn Smithyman

Editors
Molly Aloian
Kristina Lundblad

Design
Katherine Kantor

Cover design and series logo
Samantha Crabtree

Production coordinator
Katherine Kantor

Photo research
Crystal Foxton

Consultant
Patricia Loesche, Ph.D., Animal Behavior Program,
Department of Psychology, University of Washington

Illustrations
Barbara Bedell: pages 3 (fish-all except top right, sea horse, coral, shark, and
    sea fan), 4 (fish-all except blue fish and sea horse), 5 (all except top right fish),
    9 (manatee and shark), 11 (shark and fish-bottom), 13 (zooxanthellae), 20,
    24 (bottom left and bacteria), 25, 27 (all except blue fish and background), 31
Tammy Everts: page 3 (sea fan)
Katherine Kantor: pages 4 (map and blue fish), 10 (fish-top), 11 (fish-top), 12,
    24 (shark), 27 (blue fish)
Cori Marvin: pages 3 (fish-top right), 5 (fish-top right), 10 (fish-bottom)
Margaret Amy Reiach: series logo illustration, pages 3 (sea turtle, plants, clams, and
    octopus), 9 (sun and plant), 10 (plant), 11 (sea turtle and plants), 13 (magnifying glass),
    24 (plants and magnifying glass), 27 (background)
Bonna Rouse: pages 3 (starfish), 4 (starfish)
Tiffany Wybouw: page 15

Photographs
Kathy Boast - www.kathyboast.com: page 15
Seapics.com: ©David Wrobel: page 14 (bottom); ©James D. Watt:
    page 17 (bottom); ©Dave Forcucci: page 29 (top)
Visuals Unlimited: Hal Beral: page 21 (left)
Other images by Corbis, Corel, and Digital Stock

Crabtree Publishing Company

www.crabtreebooks.com   1-800-387-7650

Copyright © **2005 CRABTREE PUBLISHING COMPANY.**
All rights reserved. No part of this publication may be
reproduced, stored in a retrieval system or be transmitted in
any form or by any means, electronic, mechanical, photocopying,
recording, or otherwise, without the prior written permission
of Crabtree Publishing Company. In Canada: We acknowledge the
financial support of the Government of Canada through the Book
Publishing Industry Development Program (BPIDP) for our
publishing activities.

Cataloging-in-Publication Data
MacAulay, Kelley.
    Coral reef food chains / Kelley MacAulay & Bobbie Kalman.
        p. cm. -- (The food chains series)
    Includes index.
    ISBN-13: 978-0-7787-1948-9 (RLB)
    ISBN-10: 0-7787-1948-0 (RLB)
    ISBN-13: 978-0-7787-1994-6 (pbk.)
    ISBN-10: 0-7787-1994-4 (pbk.)
    1. Coral reef ecology--Juvenile literature. 2. Food chains (Ecology)--
Juvenile literature. I. Kalman, Bobbie. II. Title.
    QH541.5.C7M34 2005
    577.7'8916--dc22
                                                                    2005000489
                                                                          LC

**Published in
the United States**
PMB16A
350 Fifth Ave.
Suite 3308
New York, NY
10118

**Published
in Canada**
616 Welland Ave.,
St. Catharines, Ontario
Canada
L2M 5V6

**Published in the
United Kingdom**
73 Lime Walk
Headington
Oxford
OX3 7AD
United Kingdom

**Published
in Australia**
386 Mt. Alexander Rd.,
Ascot Vale (Melbourne)
VIC 3032

Contents

What are coral reefs?

Coral reefs are large underwater structures. They are found in the clear, sunlit waters of **tropical oceans**. Tropical oceans are located near the **equator**, where it is always hot. Coral reefs are made up of **corals**. Corals look like plants, but they are not plants. They are groups of tiny animals called **coral polyps**.

equator

coral reefs

Simple bodies

A coral polyp has a soft, simple body. It does not even have a brain! A coral polyp's soft body looks like a tube with an opening at the end. The opening is the polyp's mouth. The mouth is surrounded by long **tentacles**. The polyp uses its tentacles to grab food.

tentacle

mouth

How reefs form

Fire coral looks like the flames of a fire.

Some coral polyps have hard outer shells called **skeletons**. Polyps that have skeletons form **hard corals**. Polyps without skeletons form **soft corals**. Only hard corals form reefs. Different hard corals form reefs of different shapes. The hard corals shown on this page are named after the shapes they resemble.

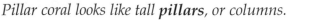

*Pillar coral looks like tall **pillars**, or columns.*

Elkhorn coral is shaped like an elk's antlers.

Many layers

When coral polyps die, their skeletons are left behind. Reefs are made up of the skeletons of these dead corals. New coral polyps then attach themselves to the skeletons and form living corals. When they die, another layer of skeletons is added to the reef. Over time, many layers of skeletons form on top of one another. It takes a long time for coral polyps to form reefs.

What is a food chain?

Plants and animals live among coral reefs. Plants and animals are living things. All living things need the same things to stay alive. They need sunlight, air, water, and food. Food helps plants and animals in two ways. First, it provides living things with **nutrients**, or substances they need to stay healthy. Second, food provides plants and animals with **energy**, which gives them power. Energy helps plants grow. Animals use energy to breathe air, to grow, and to move around.

Parrotfish bite off chunks of a reef, but they do not actually eat the reef! They eat the small plants that grow on the reef. Parrotfish have teeth in their throats that grind up the reef and separate it from the plants. After the reef is ground up, it leaves the bodies of the parrotfish as sand.

Making food

Did you know that plants make their own food? They make food using sunlight. Very few other living things can make their own food.

Eating for energy

Animals cannot make their own food using sunlight. They must eat other living things to get food energy. When animals eat other living things, a **food chain** is created. To see how a food chain works, look at the diagram on the right.

Energy from the sun

Green plants trap sunlight and turn it into food. They use some of the food and store the rest as energy.

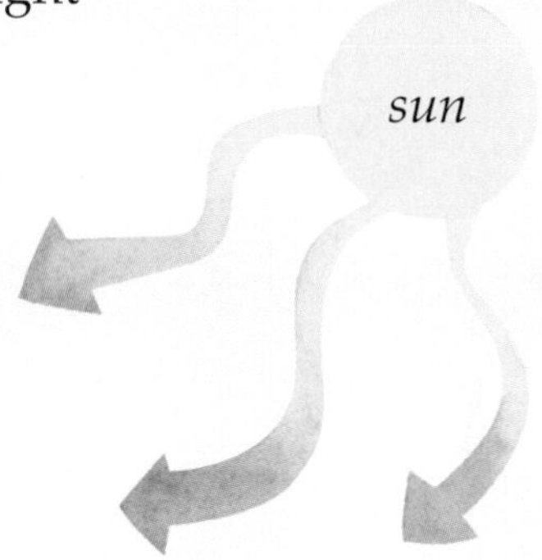

sun

plant

When an animal such as a young manatee eats a plant, it gets some of the energy that was stored in the plant. The manatee gets less of the sun's energy than the amount the plant received.

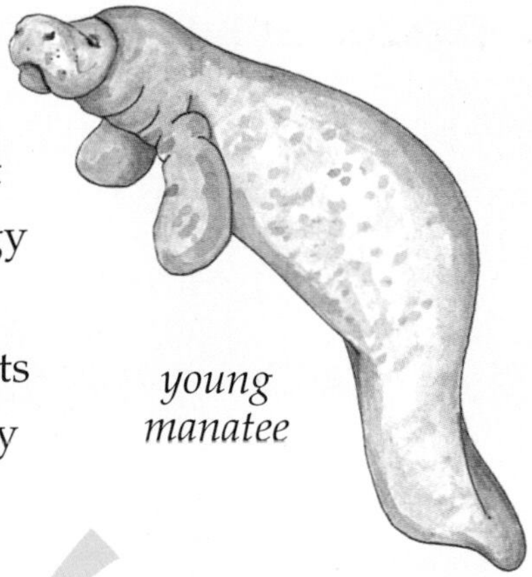

young manatee

shark

When a shark eats the young manatee, energy is passed to the shark through the plant and then the manatee. The shark gets less of the sun's energy than the amount the manatee received.

Levels of a food chain

All food chains are made up of three levels. Plants make up the first level. Animals that eat plants make up the second level, and animals that eat other animals make up the third level.

Plants make food

Plants are **primary producers**. They are the **primary**, or first, links in a food chain. They **produce**, or make, their own food. Plants store the food they do not use as energy.

Herbivores eat plants

The second level of a food chain is made up of **herbivores**, or animals that eat plants. Herbivores are also called **primary consumers** because they are the first living things in a food chain that must **consume**, or eat, food. They receive some of the sun's energy stored in plants.

Carnivores eat meat

The third level of a food chain is made up of **carnivores**, or animals that eat other animals. Carnivores are called **secondary consumers** because they are the second group of living things in a food chain that must eat food. When carnivores eat herbivores or other carnivores, they get less of the sun's energy than the amount the plants or other animals received.

10

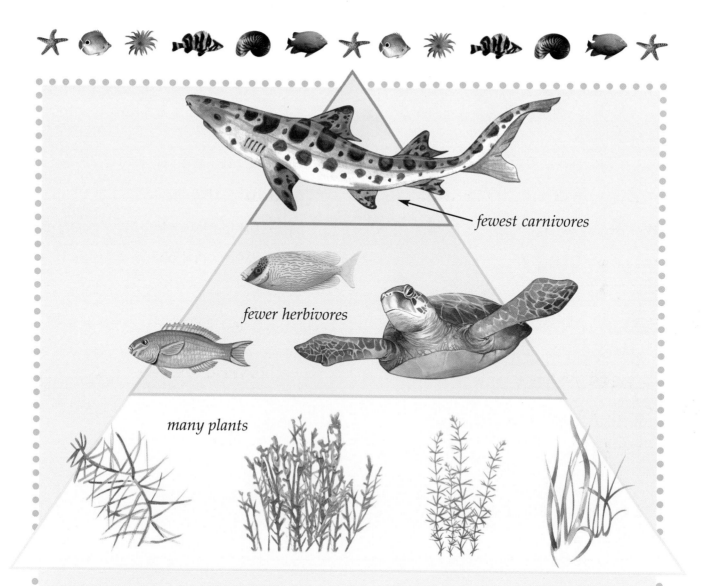

fewest carnivores

fewer herbivores

many plants

The energy pyramid

The movement of energy in a food chain is shown as a **pyramid**. A pyramid is wide at the bottom and narrow at the top. The first level of the energy pyramid is wide to show that there are many plants. It takes many plants to make food energy. The second level is narrower because there are fewer herbivores than there are plants. There are fewer herbivores because each one must eat many plants to survive. The top level of the pyramid is the narrowest because there are fewer carnivores than there are herbivores. Each carnivore must eat many herbivores to get the food energy it needs to survive.

Food from sunlight

Most ocean plants are **phytoplankton**, or tiny plants that float in oceans. They are a type of **algae**. Algae are plants that live in water. **Seaweeds** are large algae. Ocean plants make food using sunlight. Making food from sunlight is called **photosynthesis**.

As algae make food, they release **oxygen** into the ocean. Oxygen is a gas animals need to breathe. Oceans give off oxygen into the air. Oceans cover most of the Earth, and they contain a lot of algae! Algae produce most of the oxygen that ocean and land animals breathe to stay alive.

Producing food

Ocean plants contain a green **pigment**, or color, called **chlorophyll**. To make food, chlorophyll takes in sunlight. It then combines sunlight with water and **carbon dioxide**, which is a gas found in ocean water. The food plants make is **glucose**. Glucose is a type of sugar. Plants use some of the food they make and store the rest.

Sunlight shines into the shallow waters where coral reefs form.

To make food, ocean plants take carbon dioxide from the water.

As they make glucose, plants release oxygen into the water.

Feeding coral polyps

One type of algae lives inside coral polyps! **Zooxanthellae** are tiny plants that survive by being sheltered within the bodies of coral polyps. Zooxanthellae have brightly colored pigments, which give corals their beautiful colors.

As zooxanthellae perform photosynthesis, they release glucose and oxygen into the bodies of coral polyps. Coral polyps feed on the glucose and use the oxygen to breathe. Zooxanthellae and coral polyps could not survive without each other.

zooxanthellae

Feeding on plants

Coral reefs are full of life! Some coral reef animals are herbivores. **Zooplankton** are tiny animals that float in oceans. Zooplankton feed on phytoplankton. Other coral reef herbivores feed on larger ocean plants, such as seaweeds and **sea grasses**. The blue tang shown left eats different types of algae.

Sea urchins

Sea urchins are plant-eating animals that help protect coral reefs. Sea urchins feed mainly on seaweeds, and they eat a lot! Seaweeds grow quickly, however. If sea urchins did not eat seaweeds, **seaweed forests**, or large groups of seaweeds, would soon cover the reefs. When seaweed forests grow on reefs, new corals have nowhere to grow, and the reefs die.

Gentle giants

Green sea turtles are herbivores that live in coral reefs. These large animals feed mainly on seaweeds and sea grasses. They eat so many green plants that their bodies turn green! Green sea turtles have jaws that are **serrated**, or covered with sharp bumps. Having serrated jaws helps green sea turtles tear apart the plants they eat.

Some small plants grow on the shells of green sea turtles! A few types of small fish feed on these plants. The turtles provide food for the fish, and the fish clean the shells of the turtles.

15

Coral reef carnivores

Not all coral reef animals feed on plants. Many fish are carnivores that eat other animals. Some coral reef carnivores, such as sharks, are large. Others, such as the blue-banded goby shown left, are small.

Ocean predators

Many carnivores are **predators**, or animals that hunt and kill other animals for food. When a predator feeds on a herbivore, it is a secondary consumer. For example, the barracuda, shown above, is a secondary consumer when it eats a parrotfish, which is a herbivore.

When a predator feeds on another carnivore, it is a **tertiary consumer**. "Tertiary" means "third." Tertiary consumers eat secondary consumers, so they are the third group of animals in a food chain to eat. The barracuda is a tertiary consumer when it eats another carnivore, such as a grouper.

Keeping the balance

Predators are important to ocean food chains. The animals predators hunt are called **prey**. By eating prey, predators help keep the **populations** of prey animals from growing too large. If there were too many herbivores in the ocean, all ocean plants would be eaten.

Eels are hunted by sharks, but these fish have few other predators. Without sharks, the eel population would soon grow too large.

Top predators

Almost every ocean animal has predators. Large sharks, such as this tiger shark, are not hunted by other animals, however. They are the **apex**, or top, predators in oceans. Tiger sharks eat many animals, including smaller sharks, green sea turtles, and barracudas.

On the hunt

Many animals search for food in coral reefs. Some predators, such as the gopher rockfish shown left, hide among cracks in the reef. When prey swims past, the gopher rockfish darts out from the reef and grabs its prey.

A lionfish has long spines on its body that are covered with stingers. After stinging the prey with its spines, a lionfish swallows its prey whole! Groups of lionfish often hunt together for food.

Finishing the meal

Coral reef predators do not always finish their meals. Parts of dead animals, called **carrion**, drift down to the ocean floor. **Scavengers** are animals that feed on carrion. Scavengers are carnivores, but they are not predators because the food they eat is already dead.

Cleaning coral reefs

Scavengers such as lobsters, shown above, and crabs, shown left, are important animals in coral reefs. If they did not eat dead animals, the food energy stored in the carrion would be wasted. Carrion would soon pile up around the reefs! By eating carrion, scavengers help keep coral reefs clean.

The great escape

Most coral reef animals are always in danger of being eaten by predators! Over time, many animals have **adapted**, or changed, in ways that help them escape predators. For example, a butterfly fish has a spot near its tail that looks like an eye. This spot is called an **eyespot**. The eyespot fools predators into attacking the butterfly fish's tail instead of its head! When the butterfly fish sees the predator coming at its tail, it quickly swims away.

Let go!

Octopuses have many ways of escaping predators. Most octopuses can shoot clouds of inklike fluids out of their bodies. Ink clouds confuse predators, giving octopuses time to swim away. Some octopuses hide themselves by changing the color of their skin to match their surroundings. Other types of octopuses can even **detach**, or remove, their own arms if they are caught by predators! The octopuses later grow new arms.

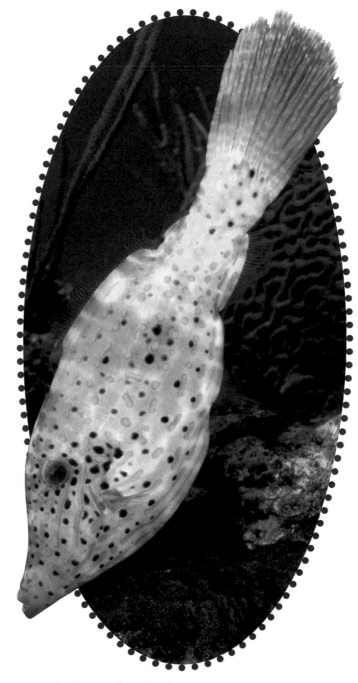

As it searches for food, a scrawled filefish floats upside down to confuse predators. Most predators believe the fish's tail is actually a piece of floating seaweed!

Coral reef omnivores

Sea fans look like plants, but they are actually animals. Sea fans are omnivores that eat tiny plants and animals.

Some coral reef animals eat both plants and animals. Animals that get food energy by eating both plants and animals are called **omnivores**. Omnivores find food easily because they are **opportunistic feeders**. Opportunistic feeders are animals that eat any food that is available.

Some omnivores eat other omnivores. A porcupine fish, shown above, eats algae. It also eats many kinds of animals, including the tube sponge shown left. Tube sponges are also omnivores.

Helping each other

Sea anemones and clown
fish are coral reef omnivores
that help each other stay alive.
The sea anemones provide safe
places among their tentacles for
the clown fish to live. Clown
fish chase away the predators
of sea anemones. Clown fish
also eat the foods left behind
by the sea anemones.

"You can't sting me!"

The tentacles of sea anemones
are covered with stingers. Sea
anemones use their stingers to
stun small fish for eating. The
stingers of sea anemones do
not harm clown fish, however.
The bodies of clown fish are
covered with thick slime,
which stops the clown fish
from feeling the stings.

Decomposers

Dead plants and animals that are **decomposing**, or breaking down, still contain nutrients. Decomposing plants and animals are called **detritus**. Living things that eat detritus are called **decomposers**. By eating detritus, decomposers release the leftover nutrients back into the water, where they can be used by growing plants.

Ocean decomposers

Most decomposers in the ocean are types of **bacteria**. Bacteria are tiny living things that are part of detritus food chains, such as the one shown right.

A detritus food chain

When a plant or an animal such as this shark dies, it becomes dead material in the ocean.

Decomposers, such as these bacteria, live in oceans. Decomposers eat the dead material and get some of the nutrients stored in it. Decomposers release some of the nutrients back into the water.

The nutrients released into the water by decomposers help new plants grow.

Note: The arrows point toward the living things that receive energy.

A healthy food chain

Decomposers are important parts of all food chains. They help keep oceans full of the nutrients that plants need in order to grow. If plants did not grow, many coral reef herbivores would starve. Without herbivores, carnivores would soon starve, too! By helping plants grow, decomposers help all levels of food chains.

Decomposers are food, too! Animals such as this tube sponge eat bacteria.

By releasing nutrients into the water, decomposers help plants grow. These plants provide food for the many animals that live in coral reefs.

A web of life

A single food chain includes plants, a herbivore, and a carnivore. Just as you eat many kinds of foods, coral reef animals eat different kinds of plants and animals. As a result, most plants and animals belong to more than one food chain. When an animal from one food chain eats a plant or an animal from another food chain, two food chains connect. When two or more food chains connect, a **food web** is formed.

A coral reef food web

The diagram on this page shows a coral reef food web. The arrows point toward the living things that are receiving energy.

A shark eats blue tangs, damselfish, and barracudas.

A barracuda eats blue tangs and damselfish.

A damselfish also eats the algae that grow on corals.

A blue tang eats the algae that grow on corals.

corals

Coral reefs in danger

Coral reefs all over the world are in danger. People are the greatest threats to coral reefs. Coral reefs look like strong walls of rock, but they can be damaged easily. Parts of coral reefs often break into pieces when they are hit by boats. People also break off pieces of coral reefs to sell as decorations for fish tanks. When people take pieces of coral reefs, they destroy the homes of many animals.

Overfishing

Many people **overfish** animals that live in coral reefs. To overfish means to take too many of one type of animal from an area. Overfishing can be harmful to many food webs. If one animal is removed from a food web, many other animals are affected. For example, many people overfish sea horses, such as the one shown right. When sea horses disappear from a coral reef, animals such as crabs, turtles, and sea lions have less food to eat. Many of these animals may starve.

Coral bleaching

Coral bleaching happens when corals lose their zooxanthellae. Without zooxanthellae, corals turn white, as shown right, and cannot catch enough food to survive. The corals soon die. Scientist believe that **water pollution** is one cause of coral bleaching. Water pollution is waste and chemicals that people dump into oceans.

Poison spreads along many ocean food chains. When a fish, such as this rock hind, eats poisoned fish, it becomes poisoned, too. If a barracuda eats a poisoned rock hind, it also becomes poisoned.

Poisoning coral reefs

Some coral reef fish are sold in fish stores. When people dive to catch the fish, most fish hide in holes on the reef. To force the fish out of the holes, some divers shoot poison into the holes. Many fish die right away from the poison. The fish that survive are taken to fish stores. Most of these fish die a few weeks later because there is poison in their bodies.

Caring for coral reefs

Prevent poisoning

You may not live near coral reefs, but you can still help save them. If you have a fish tank, never buy corals or coral reef animals for your tank. By refusing to buy corals or coral reef animals, you help prevent people from damaging or poisoning coral reefs.

Clean oceans

To help prevent coral bleaching, do not throw garbage or other pollution into rivers or streams. You can also ask your parents not to use **pesticides** on your lawn. When it rains, pesticides wash into rivers and streams. Eventually, this pollution flows into the oceans.

Visiting a reef

If you and your family ever visit a coral reef, make sure everyone knows not to touch the reef or the animals that live there. Many animals such as coral polyps are very sensitive, and even the slightest touch can kill them. It can also be dangerous for people to touch coral reef animals—many of them sting and bite!

Glossary

Note: Boldfaced words that are defined in the text may not appear in the glossary.

carbon dioxide A gas in air or water needed by plants to make food

coral reefs Large underwater structures that are built up by the skeletons of coral polyps

equator An imaginary line around the center of the Earth

oxygen A gas in air and water that animals need to breathe

pesticide A chemical sprayed on plants to kill insects

pigment A natural color found in plants and animals

population The total number of a type of plant or animal living in a certain place

sea grass A green plant that grows in oceans

tentacle A long body part used by coral polyps to grab food

Index

1 2 3 4 5 6 7 8 9 0 Printed in the U.S.A. 4 3 2 1 0 9 8 7 6 5